C000151724

Poetry for Students, Volume 24

Project Editor: Ira Mark Milne

Editorial: Jennifer Greve

Rights Acquisition and Management: Beth Beaufore, Aja Perales, Kelly Quin, Robyn Young Manufacturing: Drew Kalasky

Imaging and Multimedia: Lezlie Light Product Design: Pamela A. E. Galbreath, Jennifer Wahi Vendor Administration: Civie Green

Product Manager: Meggin Condino

For more information, contact
Gale
27500 Drake Rd.
Farmington Hills, MI 48331-3535
Or you can visit our Internet site at

attention of the publisher and verified to the satisfaction of the publisher will be corrected in future editions.

EDITORIAL DATA PRIVACY POLICY

Does this publication contain information about you as an individual? If so, for more information about our editorial data privacy policies, please see our Privacy Statement at www.gale.com.

ISBN-13: 978-0-7876-8717-5
ISBN-10: 0-7876-8717-0
eISBN-13: 978-1-4144-2935-9
eISBN-10: 1-4144-2935-5
ISSN 1094-7019

Printed in the United States of America
10 9 8 7 6 5 4 3 2 1

Ozymandias

Percy Bysshe Shelley 1818

Introduction

Percy Bysshe Shelley wrote "Ozymandias" in 1817, and it was first published in the *Examiner* in 1818. It first appeared in book form in Shelley's *Rosalind and Helen, A Modern Eclogue; with Other Poems* (1819). In the poem, the narrator relates what someone else described to him about pieces of a broken statue lying in a desert. Once a great symbol of power and strength, the statue has become a metaphor for the ultimate powerlessness of man. Time and the elements have reduced the great statue to a pile of rubble. "Ozymandias" describes an unusual subject matter for Shelley, who usually wrote about Romantic subjects such as love, nature, heightened emotion, and hope. But Shelley was also a political writer, and "Ozymandias" provides insight into the poet's views on power, fame, and political legacy. Ultimately, the poem shows that political leadership is fleeting and forgotten, no matter how hard a ruler may try to preserve his own greatness. This poem is widely anthologized, and is featured in the Norton Critical Edition (2nd edition) of Shelley's work titled *Shelley's Poetry and Prose* (2002).

Shelley kept company with an impressive array of writers, poets, and philosophers in his day. Among these was a poet and novelist named Horace Smith, whom Shelley admired for his ability to write and effectively manage his money. It was not uncommon for poets at this time to challenge each other to contests in which the two poets would select a topic or title, write their individual poems, and submit them to some sort of judging, often publication. Shelley and Smith agreed to write separate poems inspired by a passage they read by the Greek historian Diodorus Siculus. They agreed to write their sonnets about Ozymandias and submit them (with pen names) for publication. Shelley's sonnet was published first, followed by Smith's submission the next month. Today, Shelley's "Ozymandias" is one of his most famous poems.

Author Biography

Shelley was born on August 4, 1792, to Sir Timothy and Elizabeth Shelley in Sussex, England. He was one of six children, of whom he was the eldest brother. Shelley's halcyon days at the family estate did not prepare him for the bullying by other boys at Syon House Academy, in which he enrolled in 1802. Still, he gained a love for, and education in, sciences such as astronomy and chemistry.

At the age of twelve, Shelley entered Eton College, an elite boys school whose students were drawn from the British aristocracy. During his teenage years, Shelley found that he was very interested in romance. Not surprisingly, love and writing became intertwined in his literary style. His first poetry was published in 1810, as was his first Gothic novel, *Zastrozzi*.

In 1810, Shelley entered University College in Oxford. While studying at Oxford (a one-year stint), Shelley continued to pursue publication. In 1811, the publication of *The Necessity of Atheism* destroyed his family relationships. After expulsion from Oxford, Shelley wrote little and then eloped with sixteen-year-old Harriet Westbrook in August 1811.

Encouraged to pursue writing, Shelley became focused on political and religious subjects. His pamphlets reflect the influence of writers like Jean-Jacques Rousseau and Thomas Paine. Shelley also wrote personal and emotional poems that he kept in a private journal. During 1812 and 1813, Shelley and Harriet visited London, where Shelley connected with friends, publishers, and literary figures. Among these was William Godwin, a radical philosopher Shelley admired. Godwin and his deceased wife (Mary Wollstonecraft) had three daughters, all of whom fell for Shelley; but Shelley fell in love with Mary, the youngest. Outraged and heartbroken, Harriet refused an open marriage and abandoned Shelley. He and Mary ran away together on July 27, 1814, enjoying six weeks in Europe before returning home when they ran out of money. Shunned upon their return, Shelley had to work hard to earn money for himself and Mary. In November, Mary gave birth to a son named Charles. When Shelley's grandfather died in January, Shelley inherited a substantial sum of money. With the couple's financial situation now greatly improved, Shelley was free to focus on his poetry.

In January 1816, Mary gave birth to another son, William. When Mary's sister Claire became Lord George Gordon Byron's mistress, the Shelleys went with her to Lake Geneva to see him. Byron was also a poet, and he and Shelley became fast friends, discussing poetry and philosophy. During this trip, Byron challenged everyone to write a ghost story, and Mary's story became the famed novel *Frankenstein*. Meanwhile, Shelley found the natural surroundings inspiring to his poetic spirit.

The Shelleys' return to England brought the tragic news of the suicides of Mary's other sister and of Harriet. Harriet's death led to lengthy court proceedings concerning their children, who were ultimately placed with a guardian. Shelley married Mary on December 30, 1816. They moved to Marlow, where the environment suited Shelley's writing muse, and the couple interacted with such writers as John Keats and Smith. Notably, "Ozymandias" was written during a sonnet contest between Shelley and Smith. Both poets' works were initially accepted for publication by the *Examiner*, although Shelley's appeared first. He wrote the poem in December, 1817, and it was printed in January, 1818. Shelley later included it in *Rosalind and Helen, A Modern Eclogue; with Other Poems*, published in 1819. A family trip to Italy in 1818 further inspired Shelley, and for the rest of his time there, he wrote more poetry and political reform treatises.

During 1822, Mary was dejected and alone. Shelley, on the other hand, was content and carefree, spending the summer sailing and writing. On July 8, however, Shelley's boat encountered a storm that killed both Shelley and his sailing companion. Their bodies were recovered ten days later. Because of Italian law, the bodies had to be cremated, and Shelley's ashes were buried near his friend Keats's remains in the Protestant Cemetery in Rome. Mary and the children returned to England.

Poem Text

I met a traveller from an antique land
Who said: Two vast and trunkless legs of stone
Stand in the desert … Near them, on the sand,
Half sunk, a shattered visage lies, whose frown,
And wrinkled lip, and sneer of cold command, *5*
Tell that its sculptor well those passions read
Which yet survive, stamped on these lifeless things,
The hand that mocked them, and the heart that fed:
And on the pedestal these words appear:
'My name is Ozymandias, king of kings: *10*
Look on my works, ye Mighty, and despair!'
Nothing beside remains. Round the decay
Of that colossal wreck, boundless and bare
The lone and level sands stretch far away.

Lines 1-2

In "Ozymandias," the reader is receiving the information of the poem second-hand. The speaker describes what someone else told him. The speaker is merely a go-between relating information from the "traveller from an antique land" to the reader. Shelley does this to increase the distance between the mighty figure that once was Ozymandias and the present. Not only does the poem describe the rubble that once was his kingdom, but the speaker is not even looking directly at the rubble. The emotional result is greatly reduced, as when a student reads about an historical event or a piece of art rather than visiting it himself.

The poem begins with the speaker saying that he met a "traveller from an antique land," which brings to mind a country like Greece or Egypt. This traveler told the speaker that, in the middle of a desert, there are pieces of an ancient statue. First, the traveler describes two huge disembodied legs.

Lines 3-5

The legs are said to be standing in the sand of the desert. Near the legs, partially buried in the sand is the statue's broken face. These two body parts—the legs and the face—are at opposite ends of the body, so the resulting image is one that is very chaotic, inhuman, and unintimidating. On the broken face, the traveler could see the expression. It was one with a frown, wrinkled lip, and a "sneer of cold command."

Lines 6-8

The sculptor was very precise in his craftsmanship, creating a very complex and realistic facial expression. The overall effect of these features is harsh. The traveler himself comments that the sculptor clearly understood the driving passion and ambition of his subject. In fact, the traveler suggests that the passions "yet survive, stamped on these lifeless things." Mindful of the lifelessness of the broken pieces of statue, the traveler can still sense the passion that the sculptor strove to preserve in the face. The traveler also notes the "hand that mocked them [the ruler's people], and the heart that fed." This refers to the power of the king's hand to gesture and give commands, all of which reinforced his position of authority over his people. His hand mocked his people; he kept them well below him so that they could not threaten him. Yet at the same time, the ruler was human. He had a heart that made sure his people were fed. Ozymandias used his power to an extent to care for the needs of his people, whether in an attempt to be a good steward of his subjects or to ensure that his rule would continue by maintaining the favor of his people.

Lines 9-11

The last thing the traveler describes about the statue is the pedestal on which it once stood. The pedestal contains the words that Ozymandias wanted to communicate to his own generation and those that would come after him; the words reflect his pride and arrogance. It reads, "My name is Ozymandias, king of kings: / Look on my works, ye Mighty, and despair!"

Lines 12-14

These words are intensely ironic and provide the springboard into most of the thematic material of the poem. After all, as the traveler describes, all around the pedestal is nothingness. A "colossal wreck" of an old statue surrounded by endless sand is all that remains. The landscape is vast and barren.

Power

"Ozymandias" is a political poem about the illusion of fame and power. In the poem, Ozymandias was so proud of his own power and so bent on asserting it that he commissioned a great sculpture of himself glorifying his own authority. He must have believed that his political (and, given the time in which the sculpture would have been made) military power was an integral part of his own identity and purpose; after all, the way he chose to be depicted in the sculpture has all the hallmarks of strong rulership. The face is stern and resolute, appearing to be unswayed by anyone with less power than he. The hand keeps his people humble, yet Ozymandias is also the one who ensures that his people are fed. His power is such that his people seemingly would not be able to provide for their own needs without him. In all, the figure of Ozymandias is a commanding and powerful one.

The depiction of power is only part of Shelley's intent in the poem, however, and not even the most important part. More important to Shelley is showing how this great and mighty authority figure is ultimately reduced to rubble. The power he once possessed is long gone by the telling of the poem, and Ozymandias's great monument to his fame as a ruler is eroded by time and the elements. Ozymandias is no longer an intimidating figure at all, and he commands no respect from the "traveller from an antique land," the speaker, or the reader.

Topics for Further Study

- Read about the pyramids and the Sphinx in Egypt to learn what their purpose was and why they were built on such an enormous scale. Also, see what you can find out about the adverse effects of the desert climate on these ancient monuments. How are historians and archaeologists taking measures to preserve them? Based on your findings, write a script that could be used by tour guides.

- Choose another of Shelley's famous poems (such as "Hymn on

Intellectual Beauty," "Ode to the West Wind," "Mont Blanc," or "To a Skylark") and compare and contrast it to "Ozymandias." Prepare a lesson plan that leads your fellow students through the two poems, suggests conclusions, and prompts the students to make their own observations.

- Using an art form of your choice (painting, sketching, sculpture, digital, etc.), illustrate "Ozymandias." Your depiction should accurately follow the information contained in the poem, although you may take artistic license with additional details or elements.

- What would the adherents of the movement known as literary realism have had to say about this poem? Research the realists' literary point of view, take on the persona of a realistic critic, and write a review of "Ozymandias."

Pride

Akin to the theme of power is the theme of pride. Ozymandias was clearly a proud ruler who seems to have been as determined to hold onto power as he was to proclaim it to all generations. There were numerous rulers throughout history who possessed strength, stability, wisdom, and the respect of their people and other nations, and some of them felt compelled to glorify themselves in art and architecture, as did Ozymandias. While it is possible that the statue described in the poem could have been commissioned by someone other than the king, the traveler indicates that the sculptor knew his subject well. The sculptor was clearly close to Ozymandias, given access to his motives and leadership style in a way that enabled him to carve a realistic face, and to understand the symbolism of the king's hand and heart. These clues lead to the conclusion that Ozymandias oversaw the sculpture, or at the very least, the artist was caught up in the king's pride. Either way, Ozymandias's pride is clearly reflected in the statue.

Ozymandias's pride is also evident in the inscription on the pedestal. It reads, "My name is Ozymanidas, king of kings: Look on my works, ye Mighty, and despair!" This assertive statement to other mighty men is swollen with pride. He calls himself "king of kings," indicating that he sees himself as the greatest of all kings. Then he tells the viewer to observe all he has done and realize that he (the viewer) is tiny in comparison. The viewer's reaction is supposed to be utter despair at his own inferiority. Of course, Ozymandias had this inscription placed on a statue that was intended to last for hundreds of years, reminding future generations of his greatness, power, and accomplishments.

History

"Ozymandias" is a bit of history told by a traveler to the speaker, who then tells it to the reader. It has a strong tie to the oral tradition that has kept literary and historical traditions and lessons alive for hundreds of years. This fact alone prompts the reader to look for an historical lesson in the poem. The lesson reveals itself early; the poem is a cautionary tale about the transitory nature of rulers and their nations. After all, not only is Ozymandias gone, but so is the rest of his particular slice of civilization. The poem is a reminder of the historical reality of cycles of authority and the rise and fall of nations. Because the statue is from an ancient civilization, and others have come and gone between Ozymandias and the speaker's present, the reader can cull a historical lesson. Present-day readers would be wise to learn from Ozymandias and not repeat his mistake of allowing pride to seduce him into believing that his greatness would be admired forever. The poem also demonstrates that tyrannical rulers are nothing new, and that this tendency in man should be watched for among those in power.

Style

Sonnet

"Ozymandias" was the result of a sonnet competition with Smith. Shelley succeeded in containing his expression within the confines of the sonnet; the poem is fourteen lines of iambic pentameter, which are very traditional elements. Shelley breaks from tradition in his rhyme scheme, however. Rather than adhere to the English or Petrarchan rhyme schemes, Shelley does something different in "Ozymandias." The rhyme scheme is ABABACDCEDEFEF. What is interesting about this rhyme scheme is that it reinforces the subject and theme of the poem. Many skilled poets create verse that is so well-crafted that every element seems to strengthen the work, and Shelley is no exception. Here, the rhyme scheme actually evolves from start to finish. There is not a rhyme scheme separating an octave and a sestet; there is not a change at the end to finish with a neat couplet. The rhyme scheme of "Ozymandias" gradually changes over time, just as the subject matter (Ozymandias's statue) does. The last two lines have little in common with the first two, just as the rubble of Ozymandias's statue has little in common with the original structure. In both cases, the form is entirely different; only the subject is the same.

Metaphor

"Ozymandias" is at heart a metaphor. The statue represents the kings and kingdoms of the past, subject to the ravages of time, nature, and their own failings. The description of the statue and its inscription reveals tremendous pride and lost power. The statue, once magnificent, lies in ruins in the middle of a desert. It is a metaphor for all kingdoms, which eventually pass out of time to make room for another kingdom, ruler, or ideology. Shelley demonstrates that nothing lasts forever, even a ruler as powerful and fearsome as Ozymandias.

Irony

The inscription and placement of the statue brings a strong sense of irony to the poem. Although in its heyday, the statue's warning to look at Ozymandias's works and despair would have struck fear and reverence into the hearts of on lookers, the setting in the poem is quite different. The inscription reads, "Look on my works, ye Mighty, and despair!" Now, the works are gone and nothing remains but a landscape of endless sand. There are no buildings, monuments, military regiments, or palaces. The "works" seem to be wind and sand—hardly a cause for despair and terror. Ozymandias's pride appears foolish in this setting, and he seems to invite the mocking that he once doled out to his people. It is also ironic that the works that have survived all these years are not

Ozymandias's works at all, but the artist's.

Historical Context

Romantic Movement

The Romantic Movement in England took place between the publication of William Wordsworth's *Lyrical Ballads* in 1798 and the death of Charles Dickens in 1870. This was during difficult and uncertain times, as the Napoleonic Wars were underway, England faced financial difficulties, the Industrial Revolution brought both hope and despair, and new philosophies such as utilitarianism were finding a voice.

The Romantics elevated the perceived value of the individual, as well as of nature and the wild. Romantic writers tended toward emotional expression that often cycled between ecstasy and despair. The Romantics had an interest in history and mysticism. Symbolism finds its way into much Romantic literature, and writers favored imagination over realism. Although optimism and hope characterized much Romantic literature, cynicism was sometimes expressed in satire. The optimism of the Romantics was not always passive, however, and many who were attracted to the Romantic mindset were more easily swept up in movement for reform and rebellion. Byron, for example, fought for Italy against Austria, and later went to fight against the Turks with Greece for independence. He died in Greece from illness during the war.

Romantic poetry is regarded by many readers as the most accessible and beautiful of the Romantic literature. The dominant Romantic poets were Shelley, Wordsworth, Keats, Byron, Samuel Taylor Coleridge, Robert Browning, Matthew Arnold, and Lord Alfred Tennyson. Of course, the Romantic novelists produced some of the greatest works of fiction; they include Dickens, Jane Austen, Emily and Charlotte Brontë, William Makepeace Thackeray, and George Eliot. The atmosphere of debate, reform, and philosophical inquiry led to an outpouring of criticism and social commentary by writers such as Godwin, John Stuart Mill, and John Ruskin.

Ramses II

Most literary scholars agree that "Ozymandias" is based on the ancient Egyptian ruler Ramses II, or Ramses the Great (1302-1213 B.C.E.). Smith and Shelley had read about him from the work of the Greek historian Diodorus Siculus, who related an inscription describing Ramses as a great king whose works could not be surpassed. As a ruler, Ramses is remembered for his many imposing monuments, as well as for his roles as warrior, king, and peacemaker who made Egypt a world power again. In the years before Ramses's reign, Egypt lacked timber resources and other materials possessed by neighboring lands. Egypt was also politically and militarily weakened, and thus was vulnerable to being invaded and overtaken. Because of these threats to the kingdom, Ramses's father (the pharaoh) had his son trained in battle and military leadership. When he was twenty-five years old, Ramses became pharaoh following his father's death.

In ancient Egypt, the pharaoh held absolute power, although he was expected to rule and treat his people honorably. Ramses was determined to be a monument builder and make a name for himself. He went so far as to remove the names of other pharaohs on existing monuments and replace them with his own name. Ramses's works indicate that he associated himself with the sun god, Ra. The sun imagery compelled the Egyptians to give Ramses greater loyalty. Historians and archaeologists consider the two rock-cut temples at Abu Simbel to be among Ramses's most impressive surviving structures. The temple of Amun-Ra and Ramses features four sixty-seven-foot tall statues of Ramses. In the thirty-first year of his reign, however, an earthquake struck, destroying the top half of one of the statues.

Ramses even sought to construct a new Egyptian capital near his birthplace in the eastern Delta. The city was named "Domain of Ramses Great-of-Victories," but little of the city remains today. Another interesting historical feature of Ramses's construction efforts were battle reliefs. Although Ramses was a skilled and courageous warrior and general who saw many victories, he also suffered military defeats and land losses. But reading the reliefs, an observer would believe that Ramses had handily defeated his enemies in every battle.

Ramses is remembered as a powerful and accomplished king who brought strength and stability to Egypt. He was skilled at international relations, while also reinforcing his status among his own people. He died after sixty-seven years of rule. He was buried in the Valley of the Kings, but robbers stole from, desecrated, and burned the tomb. After being rewrapped and then moved twice, the mummy of Ramses is now in Cairo's Egyptian Museum.

Critical Overview

Among critics and readers, "Ozymandias" has been a favorite. Critics note that although it is something of a departure from Shelley's poetry, it is in line with his political writings. They also find the poem accessible and easily understood as the cautionary tale that it is. Critics familiar with Shelley's work as a whole are aware that Shelley's political writings were biting and called for reform. He had no sympathy for injustice or authoritarian rule, so his depiction of Ozymandias's crumbling legacy is certainly expressive of his views of politics. Writing in *ELH*, Christopher R. Miller identifies the deep cynicism of the poem when he writes, "'Ozymandias' might as well be the name for an obsolete god rather than an earthly monarch, and Shelley is really dismissing both: gods bowed to as monarchs, and tyrants worshipped as gods."

Compare & Contrast

- **1817:** Shelley's "Ozymandias" describes the ruins of a statue of a once-great leader. The expression on the statue's face and the threatening inscription demonstrate the power and harshness of the ruler.

   Today: Saddam Hussein was executed on December 30, 2006, and the war for Iraqi freedom continues after years of struggle. People all over the world still remember the image, in April 2003, of American troops toppling a twenty-foot tall statue of Saddam in Baghdad. Saddam had fled the city, and bringing down the statue represented the destruction of Saddam's reign in Iraq.

- **1817:** The Romantic Period in England is dominated by poets and novelists. Poetry is read widely and appreciated by readers from all segments of society. England takes great pride in its rich poetic heritage, and the Romantic Period became a particularly vibrant movement in this area.

   Today: Readers who choose to read poetry for leisure represent a small percentage of readership. Although students are still exposed to a wide variety of poetry in high school and college, the reading population (which is on the decline) is more interested in fiction and nonfiction than in poetry.

- **1817:** Artifacts from Egypt are just making their way to England in a traveling exhibit. The Romantic Period is characterized by a degree of interest in history, and this atmosphere generates interest in such artifacts. Until now, educated people like Shelley have only read about ancient civilizations in books and learned about them in lectures.

Today: Archaeologists have made major strides in the last 200 years, and most major cities have Egyptian artifacts in their museums. In the 1990s, there was a major traveling exhibit of artifacts from Ramses II's reign.

While commentators are drawn into Shelley's imagery and layers of meaning, it is the message inadvertently sent through time by Ozymandias that has inspired the most critical commentary. Miller states pointedly that the poem "concerns not only the physical ruins of a statue, but also the historical eclipse of a name." In *Magill Book Reviews*, a critic remarks about Ozymandias that "he is to be pitied, if not disdained, rather than held in awe and fear." The critic further observes that Shelley's message is that "the forces of mortality and mutability, described brilliantly in the concluding lines, will erode and destroy all our lives." John Rodenbeck reaches the same conclusion in *Alif: Journal of Comparative Poetics:*

> In Shelley's ... view of history, all empires are foredoomed to disappear

and for a work of what we call art merely to have outlived one of them hardly signifies anything. If that work is merely a portrait of a tyrant, moreover, the value one places upon it ... may well be largely ironical, the irony being present or absent precisely to the degree that the tyranny it was originally supposed to memorialize is in fact remembered at all.

In some ways, the message of "Ozymandias" is to be an encouragement to those who are suffering under an unjust regime, or who are angered by one. Rodenbeck remarks, "What it seeks to remind its readers, instead, is that no tyrannical power lasts forever, no matter how efficient its repressive apparatus or how deep its degree of self-deceit."

Sources

Greenfield, John R., "Percy Bysshe Shelley," in *Dictionary of Literary Biography*, Volume 96, *British Romantic Poets, 1789-1832*, edited by John R. Greenfield, Gale Research, 1990, pp. 308-38.

Harmon, William, and Hugh Holman, "Romantic Period in English Literature," in *A Handbook to Literature*, Prentice Hall, 2003, pp. 448-49.

Miller, Christopher R., "Shelley's Uncertain Heaven," in *ELH*, Vol. 72, No. 3, Fall 2005, p. 577-603.

Review of "Ozymandias," in *Magill Book Reviews*, September 15, 1990.

Rodenbeck, John, "Travelers from an Antique Land: Shelley's Inspiration for 'Ozymandias,'" in *Alif: Journal of Comparative Poetics*, Vol. 24, Annual 2004, pp. 121-50.

Shelley, Percy Bysshe, "Ozymandias," in *Percy Bysshe Shelley: Selected Poems*, edited by Stanley Applebaum, Dover Publications, 1993, p. 5.

Further Reading

Bloom, Howard, *Percy Bysshe Shelley*, Chelsea House, 1985.

> One of America's preeminent literary scholars walks students through Shelley's works with an eye toward historical and cultural context, literary status, and the Romantic personality. It includes a brief biography and a chronology to aid in research.

Godwin, William, *The Anarchist Writings of William Godwin*, Freedom Press, 1986.

> Godwin was a major influence on Shelley's thinking, and he was also his father-in-law. Although Shelley put many of Godwin's ideas into action in his life, Godwin did not always approve. This book explains Godwin's radical ideas and philosophies.

Hogg, Thomas Jefferson, *Life of Percy Bysshe Shelley*, Scholarly Press, 1971.

> Hogg and Shelley met at Oxford and were lifetime friends, despite some major challenges along the way. Here, Hogg shares his personal memories and recollections of his

friend.

Shelley, Mary Wollstonecraft, *Frankenstein*, W.W. Norton, 1996.

> Mary Shelley came up with the idea for the classic novel while in Lake Geneva with her husband, her sister, and Lord Byron. This edition contains the entire novel, along with important explanations, maps, reactions, interpretations, and critical viewpoints.

Lightning Source UK Ltd.
Milton Keynes UK
UKHW021018200820
368550UK00018B/2186

9 781375 399814